Dear Diary

An Introduction to Spiritual Journalling

by
Lawrence Osborn
A research student in theology at King's College, London

GROVE BOOKS LIMITED
Bramcote   Nottingham   NG9 3DS

CONTENTS

ACKNOWLEDGEMENTS

I am grateful to the members of the Spirituality Group for this opportunity to put my ideas about journalling onto paper and for their advice during the preparation of this booklet; thanks also to my wife, Diana, for her constructive criticism and tolerance; and, finally, thanks to Miss Kathryn Ede for her help with the cover design.

First Impression May 1988

ISSN 0262–799X

ISBN 1 85174 083 X

INTRODUCTION

'Saturday, December 14th
Feel led to keep a diary. A sort of spiritual log for the benefit of
others in the future. Each new divine insight and experience will
shine like a beacon in the darkness!

Can't think of anything to put in today.

Still, tomorrow's Sunday. Must be something on a Sunday,
surely?' [1]

Adrian Mole and his religious counterpart, Adrian Plass, have come to symbolize all that is worst in the keeping of diaries. There is a widespread suspicion that anyone who admits to keeping a journal thinks too highly of his or her own inner thoughts. By the same token many who might benefit from keeping one are discouraged by the belief that their thoughts and feelings are not worth recording.

Even so, there are many more people for whom the idea of keeping a diary is deeply attractive. A glance at the shelves of any public library or bookshop should be enough to convince anyone that the practice of keeping some form of diary or journal is by no means a novelty. One only has to think of important historical documents such as the diary of Samuel Pepys or moving accounts of the human spirit facing up to suffering, whether natural (e.g., Scott of the Antarctic) or at the hands of other humans (e.g., Etty Hillesum, Anne Frank). Virtually the entire range of human endeavour is available to us in this form, thanks simply to the incredible variety of famous and infamous men and women whose private diaries have been published (with or without their consent!).

Given such diversity it owuld be surprising if some of these journals were not concerned primaily with God. In fact, it appears that the practice of keeping some sort of spiritual journal has become widespread amongst western Christians, at least since the Reformation. Examples from Roman Catholicism include Henri Nouwen's *Genesee Diary* and Thomas Merton's *Asian Journal.* The Protestant traditions can also boast a number of journals which have become spiritual classics, e.g., those of John Wesley, George Fox, and Soren Kierkegaarde), [2]

Of course the range of diaries available on the bookshelves represents only the tip of the iceberg. I suspect that most people have made at least a token effort to keep a diary at some time or another. After all, what else can one do when Aunt Annie presents you with a birthday present of a five-year diary bound in red simulated leather and 'secured' with a tiny brass padlock? Any attempt to record adolescent secrets is soon abandoned when you discover that the padlock is no deterrent to a younger brother or sister armed with a paper-clip!

[1] Adrian Plass, *Sacred Diary of Adrian Plass (aged 37¼)*, (Marshall-Pickering), p.1.
[2] A list of some of the better-known spiritual journals can be found in section (b) of Chapter 5.

In the twentieth century this long tradition of diary keeping has received fresh impetus from the development of psychoanalysis. The seminal figure is without doubt Carl Jung. His encounter with his own unconscious was aided by the keeping of a journal of his fantasies. This practice has been taken up and formalized by the American analyst. Ira Progoff, who is perhaps the chief exponent of the use of journalling as a vehicle for self-realization. A less formal approach to journalling, but one also influenced by Jung, is that of the English psychoanalyst Marion Milner. An alternative approach (which places more emphasis on the journal as an aid to personal creativity) has been inspired by the work of Otto Rank. It reaches its clearest literary expression in *The Diary* of Anais Nin, and an account of this approach can be found in the work of her disciple and colleague Tristine Rainer.

The result of this interest in journals from psychoanalysts has been the discovery (or rediscovery) that the journal can be an important tool in the search for selfhood in our increasingly fragmented society: a search which for the post-war generation was symbolized by the diary of Anne Frank and which, more recently, has been parodied by Adrian Mole. Thoreau once commented that 'It is as hard to see oneself as to look backwards without turning round.' Following this hint, we might compare the role of journal with that of a mirror. Through its pages we may discover who we really are. Commenting on this diary. Henri Nouwen says

> 'I have little to say about events, good or bad, creative or destructive, but much about the way I remember them—that is, the way I start giving them form in the story of my life.'[1]

What is a Journal?
One question I ought to tackle before going any further is how a journal differs from a diary. At one level the terms are interchangeable. My dictionary defines them both as a 'daily record of events'. However, the word 'diary' suggests a pre-printed book with a fixed amount of space for each day and, perhaps, for appointments every half-hour. Bishop John Robinson described his own journal as

> 'something very different from a diary, which has always oppressed me. There you feel you have got to record something every day, whether there is something worth saying or not . . .'[2]

Because of that shade of meaning I propose to avoid the word 'diary' where possible in what follows.

What then is a journal? As I have already said, it is a mirror of the self. This mirror is created by maintaining a private record of your observations and intuitions, your thoughts and feelings, and your reflections on all of these. It is primarily, though not exclusively, about yourself. It cannot be exclusively about self for the simple reason that no-one lives an entirely isolated life. Our relationships with others play an important part in making us who we are.

[1] Henri Nouwen, *The Genesee Diary: Report From A Trappist Monastery* (Doubleday), p.160.
[2] Quoted in Eric James, *A Life of Bishop John A. T. Robinson: Scholar, Pastor, Prophet* (Collins), p 285.

The last point also suggests the main distinction between a 'spiritual' journal and a secular one. A spiritual journal is not just a book of prayers or personal Bible meditation although it may be that as well. No, the real difference lies in the realization that our relationship with God is the central factor in the discovery of self. The contents of a spiritual and a secular journal may overlap to a considerable degree. But, even when it is at its most mundane (or, perhaps, precisely then), it is written before God and in the awareness of the relationship he has established with us.

Many people already keep some form of journal. Many more have tried and failed, or are vaguely aware that other Christians seem to derive great benefit from the practice. For all who want to do more with their journal, or who would like to try again, or who would like to keep a journal but do not really know where to begin, I would like to offer some suggestions and fresh alternatives. This is first and foremost a collection of hints and further resources for the would-be journal keeper. It is not a theoretical analysis and critique of the practice of keeping a journal. Above all, it is not a rule book for 'successful' journalling: please use what you find helpful and disregard the rest.

1. GETTING STARTED

Surprising as it may seem, given the sheer quantity of published diaries, one of the major difficulties faced by many would-be diarists is the practical one. How does one actually get started with a journal? The problem is created largely by the fact that we think there is no problem. After all, is it not obvious how a diary should be kept? Any good desk diary will show you how! Imagine it sitting in front of you waiting to be used. It offers you one page per day (no more and no less) which you must fill with your words of wisdom, observations on life, reflections on God, etc. It is clearly expected that you will write more or less the same amount every day—regardless of time, physical or mental health, or inspiration.

But once you have overcome this hurdle you may well run straight into a second difficulty. You will find yourself asking, 'Is it safe to say what I think? Who might read this?'

Privacy
If the aim of keeping a journal is to reflect on your life in a very personal way then the most important point is probably to ensure the privacy of your journal. Most people involved in journalling insist on this simply because otherwise you may be tempted to write what you think others would like to read. Take whatever steps you feel are necessary to prevent others from reading and you are more likely to be honest with yourself (and God). For many years, Beatrix Potter kept a journal in a secret code of her own invention. I do not altogether recommend this practice. Although she became fluent in her code she forgot the key when her journal lapsed and in later life was quite unable to read her own notes. I might add that privacy is only the first step to honesty in a journal: the temptation to write what you like to believe about yourself still remains. Jim Elliott was very realistic in beginning his journal thus:
> 'What is written in these pages I suppose will someday be read by others than myself. For this reason I cannot hope to be absolutely honest in what is herein recorded, for the hypocrisy of this shamming heart will ever be putting on a front and dares not to have written what is actually found in its abysmal depths. Yet, I pray, Lord, that You will make these notations to be as nearly true to fact as is possible so that I may know in my own heart and be able to definitely pray regarding my gross, though often unviewed, inconsistencies.'[1]

I think Jim Elliott hit upon a key to honesty in the context of a spiritual journal. While we delude ourselves only too easily, there is no deluding God. Consciously bringing God as a partner into the journalling process, is to offer him the perfect opportunity to destroy our self-delusion.

The Type of Notebook
Next in importance after privacy is the sort of notebook you choose to keep your journal in. I would advise against the use of hardback pre-printed diaries. As I have already suggested, they both make unreasonable demands and impose unreasonable limits on your journalling. They

---

[1] E. Elliott (ed.), *The Journals of Jim Elliott* (Pickering and Inglis), p.11.

6

seem to demand some sort of entry every day and this may well create a sense of guilt when one fails to make an entry for a week or even a month. They also restrict the length of journal entries by offering a set space for each day (which may on some occasions be too little and others too much). An undated notebook is far better.

The choice of hardback or looseleaf is more a matter of personal preference. I prefer a looseleaf notebook because of its greater flexibility. However others find that a hardback enables them to keep notes in a clearer chronological order and helps them to resist the temptation to doctor the records at a later date.

Whatever your choice, make sure that your journal is both hard-wearing and portable. It must be hard-wearing to withstand regular use, possibly for many years. It must be portable to avoid the frustration of having a flash of inspiration on the top of a bus while your journal lies in a cupboard miles away.

Alternatively, you might choose to copy entries made in haste on the backs of envelopes or bus tickets into a master journal kept at home. Personally I find this approach too time-consuming and it also tempts me to edit the entries when I copy them. However, if you are happy with doing this, it opens up new possibilities in journal keeping. For example, you might like to experiment with keeping your journal on a computer. Recent developments in the field of home micros now makes it possible to store your journal in an information processing system which combines word processor with database. Nor are you confined to the written word as many home computers now allow you to store sophisticated graphics (and even video pictures).

The size of your journal is also worth thinking about. As I have already noted, if it is too large to carry about with you it is probably too large. On the other hand, if it is very small you may find yourself starting new volumes at frequent intervals. A small journal may also be a liability when it comes to reviewing: ideally it should be large enough for you to leave a generous margin for subsequent comments. Finally some journal users find that very small notebooks affect their style of writing, forcing them to write in a way that they feel to be cramped and perhaps too cryptic.

Another possibility is to keep a tape journal. This is particularly appropriate for those who cannot bear to write things down or who like to think out loud. The disadvantage is that it is cumbersome and very awkward to review. Tapes are also significantly less hard-wearing than notebooks.

The 'No-Rule' Rule

I said in the introduction that this was not a rule book. However, I make this one exception. The only rule for a successful journal is that there are no rules. In your journal you are completely free to do your own thing. To start with, this means that you need not worry about 'correct' English.

There are no limits on the content of your journal. Entries may be of any length from headlines to extended essays (the only limits being your time and inspiration). The material need not be original to you (I know of an evangelist who keeps a 'journal' consisting exclusively of personally significant quotations). You might like to paste into your journal newspaper clippings or important letters. The content need not even be written: a diary may legitimately include photographs, diagrams and sketches. If you like you may even try describing your day graphically (Carl Jung was a pioneer in this, with his use of mandalas — spontaneous geometric patterns reflecting his feelings about the day — in his journals).

As for how often one must make entries in the journal, the only rule is: whenever one feels like doing so. There is no need to keep a daily record of events. Indeed some exponents of spiritual journalling recommend that you make only two or three entries a week. If you like, the entries may be quite infrequent. One of the finest twentieth century examples of a spiritual journal (Dag Hammarskjold's *Markings*) consists largely of undated paragraphs, and those that are dated suggest that weeks or even months went by between entries. Even more extreme are some journals from mediaeval Japan: each entry was a work of art and there might have been no more than one entry in a year. It all depends on the purpose of your journal. For most people the search for personal identity and a thread of continuity in their lives will be major consideration. In such cases, frequent entries provide more raw material with which to work.

Of course, a journal need not be kept continuously. You may prefer to resort to the practice only on special occasions. For example, Marion Milner has revived the tradition of keeping a holiday journal. This may be particularly appropriate for people whose normal daily schedule leaves them little time for reflection. Transposed into a religious mode, the holiday journal becomes the retreat journal. Henri Nouwen's *Genesee Diary* is a good example of this sort of thing (and the idea is equally valid whether one has seven months to spare, like Nouwen, or just a couple of days). While on the subject of time and journalling, it may be worth pointing out that a journal entry need not be limited to today's events. If something that happened yesterday is on your mind, by all means note it down. And the same goes for something that happened last week or ten years ago. Today's memories may be of far greater significance than today's events.

By the same token, it follows that you need never worry about incompleteness. In fact, 'oversights' can often be very illuminating when they occur to you at some later date: Why didn't I make any note of that blazing row with my wife? Why do I never make any reference to X, Y or Z?

Starting to Write

Precisely because there are no rules, I am reluctant to say too much at this point. And yet, I realize that someone may be looking for some piece of advice, something to actually get them started. Perhaps the soundest response is the one which Tristine Rainer gives:

'Write fast, write everything, include everything, write from your feelings, write from your body, accept whatever comes.'[1]

It may be worth adding that a spiritual journal, since it puts our life into the context of our relationship with God, ought to be written in the context of prayer and meditation on the events of the day. My own practice, for such premeditated entries, is to spend a few minutes in silence, placing the day (or the interval since the last entry) before God. Then I begin by writing down whatever is uppermost in my mind after the period of silence. Thereafter I just let it flow.

Re-reading

As important as the entries themselves is the practice of re-reading your journal at more or less regular intervals. If you are serious about keeping a journal then you must keep this in mind. Otherwise what you do may degenerate into a meaningless daily ritual which will sooner or later fall into abeyance. Of course, you may have reasons for writing a journal which you do not wish to re-read. Some people write as part of a regular exercise of self-examination with no desire to re-read the material later. They may even destroy the material as soon as it is written. Although such a practice can obviously make use of a number of techniques associated with journalling, it is doubtful whether it can really be classified as keeping a journal.

On the matter of setting aside time for re-reading, the approach you adopt will depend very much on how your time is committed. For many people the easiest approach will probably be to set aside a short period each week to look back over what they have been entering in their journal. Others may prefer to set aside an occasional day or weekend for a more extensive examination of the contents of their journal. In addition to such regular reviews, most experienced journal users find themselves turning to their journal on special occasions. For example, the beginning of a new volume may be an appropriate time to glance back through previous volumes as may the start of a new year, a change of home or job, a birthday or some other anniversary.

Having decided to set aside time to re-read (when and how much is a purely personal matter) the question then arises of how to re-read. The secret is never to re-read your journal passively. It is not a novel in which you can simply let yourself be carried along by the author as he unfolds a carefully worked-out story line. It is more like a collection of scrappy notes, disjointed, contradictory, perhaps even unintelligible. It is raw material from which you may be able to construct something. But the

---

[1] Tristine Rainer, *The New Diary* (Angus and Robertson). p.34.

onus is on you to do something as you read. It is very unusual for an unedited journal to yield treasures without any work on your part. Active re-reading can involve all sorts of journal exercises. Some of these I describe in the concluding section and many more can be found by consulting the books referred to at the end. At this stage I will content myself with a few general suggestions.

Broadly speaking, the content of a journal can be classified into four basic types of writing corresponding to the four psychological functions described by Jung. These types are:

(a) descriptive (corresponding to sensing)

(b) brainstorming or free-intuitive writing (corresponding to intuition)

(c) reflective (corresponding to thinking)

(d) cathartic (corresponding to feeling)

According to Jung, we all make use of all four psychological functions according to a personal hierarchy of preference. It seems likely that the content of our journal will tend to reflect our preference. By noting the sort of material in our journal we may get a better idea of our own preference amongst the psychological functions. We may find that one or more of the types is conspicuous by its absence. This might prompt us to ask questions about why we are avoiding that type of writing. For example, why am I reluctant to express my feelings in the journal? Once aware of such preferences we may go on to exercise those neglected functions in our journalling.

Another approach is to listen for 'voices' in the journal. Is this my conscious self speaking? Or am I expressing what is expected of me by family, friends, or society at large? Perhaps it is not identifiable as either of these. The 'voice' I have identified may be the expression of a part of my personality of which I am not normally conscious. Whatever the source of the 'voice', Ira Progoff's dialogue technique is particularly helpful as a way of getting to know and understand it better. We shall be looking at this in more detail below.

Or you may elect to look out for patterns and rhythms in the journal. Is there a recurring dream? What about references to particular emotions: can they be correlated with events in my life?

Or again, on the borderline between the personal journal and the appointments diary, is there anything which I have conspicuously avoided? Am I procrastinating about something? Reviewing my personal journal may well form the basis for a list of things which need to be attended to.

Reviewing is also a good time for reflecting on striking dreams and fantasies. Once again Progoff's dialogue technique may be used here. Other approaches may be found by consulting some of the many works that are now available on dreams and Christian spirituality.[1]

[1] See Chapter 5, section (d), for some suggestions.

It is very helpful to devise some sort of indexing system for use at the initial review stage. Progoff does this by classifying material into different types based on his analysis of mental activity. However, what such a classification offers in the way of systematization is counterbalanced by a severe loss of continuity. It might also be worth noting that, unless you have time to spare in copying out unclear material several times to insert into different sections, such systematizing tends to oversimplify what is actually taking place.

George Simons recommends a system of marginal letter codes which works equally well with looseleaf or hardback notebooks. His own code is as follows:

C: CLUES AND HINTS (entries which record flashes of insight, interest or feeling)

IC: INNER CONVERSATIONS (points at which a 'voice' other than my conscious self appears to be expressing itself)

S: STRUGGLES, WORRIES, PROBLEMS

D: DREAMS

F: FOLLOW-UPS (entries based on reviews of earlier parts of the journal)

TD: TO DO (entries which require action)

M: MOVEMENT (entries which seem to betoken growth, new awareness, personal development)

FAN: FANTASIES, DAY DREAMS

H: PERSONAL HISTORY

MED: MEDITATIONS (also reflections, commentaries, etc.)

ST: STATEMENTS (things we ought to say to other people)

If such a system seems likely to help you, you could start by modifying the above to suit your own needs (e.g., P could indicate a prayer or petition). However, I would caution against starting with a complex system. It is far better to begin simply and allow your indexing code to grow with your journal: after all, it is intended to pick out items that are important to you.

Finally, it is important to remember that review is not the same as revision or editing. You may find yourself, two years on, cringeing with embarrassment or self-disgust at past entries. You may find yourself disagreeing strongly with former opinions. The temptation to deny the feelings and opinions of your former self is just as much a temptation to self-delusion as the temptation to write for an audience. If you cannot simply leave a past entry alone, then it is far better to add a marginal comment than to alter or delete the entry.

2. THE INTENSIVE JOURNAL

While it is true that diaries have been with us for centuries there has perhaps never before been an age when diary-keeping has been taken so seriously (and nowhere is this more true than in the United States). The recent revival in journalling is due mainly to psychoanalysis and twentieth century man's obsession with self-actualization. Journals have played a significant role in this process, ever since the analyst Carl Jung transformed the professional journal of the scientist into a vehicle for exploring the depths of his own psyche.

The most highly developed version of this is undoubtedly the intensive journal programme developed by the American psychologist Ira Progoff. For Progoff a diary is much more than a vehicle for reporting the events of one's life or even of self-expression. Rather, he hit upon the use of a journal in his quest for 'a method for actively extending life experience.'[1] If you like, it is a technique for helping to achieve self-realization.

As it now stands, the Intensive Journal comprises a variety of specialist diaries or 'logs' dealing with different aspects of the inner life. These are bound together into an organic whole by a series of journal exercises designed to stimulate the way in which creative people can experience, and integrate into a developing whole, the contents of their lives. Underlying these exercise is the assumption that such integration occurs through processes analogous to feedback between the conscious and the unconscious parts of an individual psyche.

'Feedback' is a term widely used in the world of electronic control systems to describe the return to a system or process of part of its output. Usually such techniques are used to maintain the stability of a system. It is in this sense that Progoff intends us to understand the word. The Intensive Journal allows us to articulate something of what is taking place in our subconcious. But 'feedback' implies more than this. It suggests that the exercises are so designed that the act of carrying them out in the conscious mind has an effect on the unconscious: specifically a stabilizing or self-fulfilling effect.

The most effective way of learning the techniques involved is to take part in a workshop run by Progoff or one of his students. Unfortunately there are few such workshops in the United Kingdom.[2] A much less satisfactory alternative is to work through Progoff's writing on the Intensive Journal. He attempts to simulate the presentation of his workshops. The problem is that what works in a live workshop has been transformed in the process into very repetitious and unclear prose.

An important aspect of the workshops is the stress on privacy. For Progoff this is far more than an aid to honesty in journal keeping. It is part and parcel of his rejection of dependence on others in the quest for self-fulfilment. For this reason the workshops are largely non-interactive, in

---

[1] Ira Progoff, *At a Journal Workshop* (Dialogue House), p.31.
[2] See Chapter 5, section (e), for further information.

spite of a certain amount of voluntary sharing of what one has written. Keeping a journal is seen as an exclusively individual occupation: I write on my own without the support or direction of others. The key to success, the key to fulfilment is to be found exclusively within me. Progoff believes that, 'Given the opportunity, a life crystallizes out of its own nature, revealing its meaning and its goal.'[1]

For the same reason, the workshops are quite non-directive. Participants are free to make what they will of the techniques. They are free to follow their own insights or to use the Intensive Journal in conjunction with very diverse spiritual disciplines of humanistic personal development techniques. Perhaps because he permits you to use the method in the context of your own values and beliefs. Progoff is highly regarded in America by Christians, humanists and adherents of a variety of other religions.

The starting point of the Intensive Journal is the question. 'Where am I now in my life?' The answer to this question forms the very first entry in the journal, as part of the Period Log. Progoff does not dwell on this. In the workshops, a definite time limit is placed upon this stage of the exercise. What is wanted is a brief statement uncensored by the conscious mind. From there one moves rapidly to dealing with the Period Image. This is the first encounter with the cluster of techniques which Progoff sometimes calls process meditation. Having focussed our consious minds on the present period of our lives we are encouraged to relax and enter into a meditative state. Through such meditation we contact the stream of imagery which Progoff believes forms part of our subconscious. The purpose of the Twilight Imagery Log is to collect any images which occur to us while we are in such a state.

From the Period Log we move to the Daily Log. This is the backbone of the Intensive Journal, as it is of any journal. The name is self-explanatory. It is worth noting that this is a log rather than a journal: the contents are brief, value-free descriptions of our day, of our feelings and our reactions to others:

> 'It has the function of gathering into one accessible place a running record of the subjective experiences of all kinds that move through a person's mind and emotions in the course of a day and night.'[2]

In the Journal itself, the next major division is the first of the three major dimensions of life: the Dialogue Dimension. This is essentially the section in which we may work with our relationships and experiences by a process of inner dialogue. Progoff treats this technique as central to the entire journalling process. He applies it not only to our personal relationships but also to the way we feel about our work, our leisure, our body, the events that affect us, the groups that are significant to us, society at large, and even our inner experiences. In each case the method is broadly similar. The starting point is a brief session of what might be described as brainstorming in which you compile, as rapidly as possible, a list of eight to ten items related to the development of your relationship

[1] *Journal Workshop*, p.10.
[2] Id. p.86.

with the object of the dialogue exercise (persons, works, interests, aspects of your body, etc.). The reason for speed is to encourage what Progoff calls 'spontaneous selectivity': by discouraging conscious reflection in this way you are able to arrive at a list of greater sub-conscious significance. Progoff calls these lists Steppingstones, a name which highlights their developmental nature. You then choose one item from your list and briefly summarize its major characteristics as it affects you (again the brainstorming technique is useful).

Having arrived at that summary, you enter into the twilight state of meditative relaxation. Having settled yourself into that state you are asked to feel the object of your meditation as a personal presence (this may take some getting used to if the object of your meditation is your left elbow!). Once 'in the presence' of your object, you address him, her, or it, and write down what transpires. At the end of the session, you are asked to review your feelings about the dialogue that has occurred.

The second dimension of the Intensive Journal is Depth. This section of the journal covers all your direct dealings with the largely symbolic, subconscious aspects of your experience. It is in this section that you record recollections of dreams, daydreams, fantasies, or imagery that arises as a direct result of your journalling exercises. But Progoff is not content to have us record fragments of dreams. He encourages us to enter into the twilight state described above and proceed to elaborate our recollections.

He also uses this section to record a special type of dialogue: our dialogues with our inner wisdom, our spiritual experience. These take the form of dialogues with spiritual authority figures, our gods, saints, heroes, and teachers:

> 'Whoever has spoken to us in the depth of our being, whether through their spoken words, their books, their music, their paintings, or by their lives and the legends and symbolism that have grown around them, all of these may be wisdom figures for us in some areas of our life.'[1]

In effect we are encouraged to enter into an imaginary personal relationship with our chosen 'guru'.

The final dimension of the Intensive Journal is the Life/Time Dimension. This is used to enable us to reflect on our past: the events and persons which have made us who we are; the decisions we have made; our successes and failures. Once again, we begin with a list of Steppingstones: in this case an eight- or ten-statement autobiography. By bringing the various journalling techniques to bear, we gradually elaborate on this picture. The end-result is a deepened understanding of how we have become who we are. An important aspect of this dimension is working with the unlived possibilities in our life. As we examine our life history we note the crucial decisions we have made. We enter imaginatively into the decision-making process once again. We begin to explore the possibilities of the options we have rejected. The point of this is that

> 'Abilities, projects and relationships which were roads that could not be taken in earlier years may become more feasible in a much richer way with the passage of time.'[2]

---

[1] *Journal Workshop*, p.277.
[2] *Id.*, p.138.

Critique

In spite of his dominant role in the world of journalling, Progoff's approach is not without its critics. The main criticisms of his approach focus on the relatively complex systematic structure of the Intensive Journal.

Underlying that structure is a hypothetical reconstruction of the way in which creative persons appear to deal with their inner lives. This hypothesis is not treated in sufficient detail in Progoff's works on journalling for a critique to be possible. However, the very fact that the system is built on a construct of human creativity which is not universally accepted by psychoanalysts working in this field will cause us to pause for thought. Those who disagree with the fundamental premises on which Progoff's hypothesis is constructed will be unable to adopt his system as a whole (or, if they do, it will be at the cost of considerable inner tension). This should be borne in mind by Christians considering the use of the Intensive Journal.

Another cause for concern is the very strong emphasis on self-reliance in Progoff's writings. We have already commented that, although the technique is taught in groups, the journalling experience is essentially solitary. For Progoff it appears that fulfilment is found by delving into oneself. It is certainly not to be found through dependence on others. Even God can be a hindrance: Progoff comments that a journal written with a definite goal in mind (and he cites achieving a closer relationship with God as an example) 'has the effect . . . of limiting the person.'[1]

The reason for the insistence on self-reliance is his assumption that each individual contains his own inbuilt dynamic: a natural tendency to develop in the right direction for personal self-fulfilment. Progoff's programme is designed to aid this internal process. He relies heavily on feedback between the conscious and the unconcious parts of the psyche and he assumes too readily that such a process is benign. There seems to be no recognition of the very real dangers associated with such casual explorations of the subconscious. It was precisely because of these dangers that secular psychoanalysts evolved the practice of themselves undergoing analysis as an ongoing part of their work.

Some British users of the Intensive Journal have built an extra safeguard into the system. They suggest that you should always respect your own privacy. If, in the course of a journal exercise, you feel that it would be too painful to proceed, respect that feeling. You may not be ready to tackle that issue on your own.

This criticism may be transposed to a theological level. Progoff takes no account of human sinfulness or the demonic dimension of human experience. Nor is his Intensive Journal merely a neutral technique: the claims made for it assume an unduly optimistic assessment of human nature.

Having said this, there remains much of value in Progoff's techniques which can be appropriated without taking on board his questionable assumptions about human nature. The most basic of Progoff's exercises are 'Steppingstones' and 'Dialogue'. How these may be used in a spiritual journal will be dealt with in Chapter 4.

[1] *Journal Workshop,* p.25.

3. THE JOURNAL AS AN AID TO SPIRITUAL GROWTH

In spite of Progoff's warning against starting a journal with a specific goal in mind, the Christian journal keeper will invariably want to allow God to influence his journal. His or her motive for keeping a journal will thus be significantly different from that of the non-Christian. Instead of self-realization without reference to others and by one's own efforts, the Christian's goal is better summarized in terms of imitation of Christ: of being conformed to the model presented by our Lord. The Christian's spiritual journal will reflect that concern in its special themes which we may examine under the headings of self-examination, reflection or meditation, and prayer.

The Journal as an Aid to Self-examination

The seminal work of Christian self-examination is surely the *Confessions* of St. Augustine. In fact this is neither a journal nor a true autobiography. What Augustine has done is to use autobiography as a vehicle for expounding a theology of the Christian life. Nevertheless, this work offers us a useful starting point for the Christian tradition of written self-examination. This is a tradition which transcends denominational boundaries. From popes and priests to pietists and puritans, the journal has been used as a vehicle for honest self-appraisal before God.[1]

This is probably the aspect of keeping a spiritual journal that comes closest to the intentions of the current generation of secular journal writers. Where they seek to understand themselves better in the hope of finding their salvation within, the Christian seeks a better self-understanding in the context of his of her relationship with God. Most of the techniques used in secular journalling can be adapted for use as tools of self-examination in the spiritual journal. The essential difference is the realization that in the spiritual journal they are not being used as aids in a solo voyage of self-discovery but in the context of a relationship. The Christian's journal and the exercises used in it are never written in private but always in the presence of God.

Since the goals of secular and spiritual journals diverge, the reasons for self-examination also differ. In general, secular journalling techniques stress self-examination for the purpose of discovering who you are and accepting what you discover as good and proper. Christian self-examination is bound to be more self-critical. We have already noted that the Christian's ultimate aim is conformity to the norm provided by the life of Jesus Christ. Honest self-examination will therefore recognize the points at which we fall short of this norm as failings. For this reason published spiritual journals often make quite depressing reading as the author confronts us with his sins and weaknesses.

But although the spiritual journal will contain a proportion of honest self-criticism, it ought not to be entirely negative. The only reason for highlighting our failings is so that we are in a better position to do something about them. Henry Martyn, for example, recorded not only his

[1] Many examples of this use of the spiritual journal may be found in the journals cited in Chapter 5, section (b).

besetting sins but those occasions on which he was able to resist them. The same balance of failures and victories is a common feature of spiritual journals.

Keeping such a journal is a useful spiritual discipline particularly for those whose personality type inclines them not to dwell very much on their inner lives. Developing one's inner life is an important part of spiritual growth. But the inwardness that grows out of being self-critical before God is very different from mere self-absorption. It recognizes the importance of our relationships with God and our neighbours.

One special form of self-examination that is worthy of separate note is the spiritual autobiography. In its journal form this corresponds to the Life/Time Dimension of the intensive Journal. If we may imagine the Christian life as a pilgrimage or journey, this aspect of keeping a journal resembles the drawing of a map of where we have come from. It is a way of giving form to our lives and, since the exercises and entries are written in the conscious presence of God, it will be natural to see that journey as a journey with or towards God. This does not mean that every entry is an explicit attempt to interpret the day's events as cases of divine providence or intervention. It does mean that all the mateiral is available for later searches for providential patterns. The journal may enable us to perceive God's activity in our lives and the lives of those around us.

The Journal as an aid to Reflection and Meditation
With this we come quite close to the common practice of evangelical students (and others) of keeping a written record of what they have gained from the reading of Scripture. The distinction between them lies in the greater personal emphasis of the journal. It is not meant to be a chronological commentary on one's Bible reading. The journal is the place for recording anything which is of particular personal importance. Again many examples of this type of entry may be found in the spiritual journals listed at the end.

Those who read the Bible systematically may want to do so with their journals open beside them. In addition one may want to use the journal in conjunction with other spiritual reading. Those who feel so inclined may even adapt systems such as St. Ignatius' spiritual exercises for use in the journal.

The Journal as an Aid to Prayer
The idea that the journal may be a tool for Christian meditation leads naturally to the notion of praying in and through the pages of your journal. As I have stressed throughout, the spiritual journal is written in the presence of God. At times it will seem perfectly natural not only to write in his presence but to address what you write directly to him. This may take the form of letters to God, or you may find yourself writing meditative poetry, hymns of praise, etc. Once again, Jim Elliott's journal is a good example of what may happen.

Your will certainly not want to use it as an exclusive method of prayer but it offers an interesting alternative to oral forms of prayer. At the very least it can serve as a valuable aid to concentration if you find your mind wandering when you pray. It can also be helpful in pointing out deficiencies in other aspects of your praying. Intercessory prayer is a good example. You might want to use your journal to record your prayer concerns; specific requests and answers to prayer. It can be used to clarify the matters that really concern you, to focus either the direction of your life or the emphasis in your prayers.

Closely related to prayer is the whole area of divine guidance. Once again the journal is a suitable vehicle for working out important decisions in God's presence, and recognizing retrospectively how God has helped you. This, in turn, can be a stimulus to thanksgiving and praise.

4. GOING ON

In the section that follows you will find brief descriptions of a variety of exercises which you may choose to experiment within your journal. As with any other aspect of journalling there are no rules to be followed: no right or wrong way of approaching these exericses, no right or wrong place or time to try them out. By all means try them all, or one or two that interest you (I hope there is sufficient variety here for you to find at least one or two of interest!). Further exercises and hints can be found in the books and courses described in Chapter 5.

Unsent Letters

These are just what they say they are. A letter which you have no intention of sending affords the perfect opportunity to write precisely what you feel without fear of hurting someone's feelings or facing a hostile backlash. Such letters are primarily an exercise in catharsis. If you are the sort of person who distrusts feelings or dislikes expressing them, you may find such an exericse worthwhile. The process of expressing your feelings in secret and on paper may help you to feel more at ease with them in public.

An obvious 'spiritual' corollary would be to write letters to God. What do you really feel like saying to God? Practice at expressing your feelings to God in this way may help to bring greater realism into your prayers.

Portraits

You might like to try writing imaginative descriptions of the people around you. What do they look like? How do they behave? How does their appearance and behaviour affect the way you respond to them? As you seek to understand others and your relationship with them in this way, you may well find that your relationship develops and strengthens. Another possibility might be to write a self-portrait, looking at yourself, your physical appearance, your manneriesms, or your habits.

Dialogues

The people for whom you have written journal letters or portraits are obvious candidates for this very important journalling technique. Dialogue writing was popularized by its use in Gestalt therapy and, as we have seen, has become the keystone of Progoff's Intensive Journal. However, journal keepers have long known the value of writing imaginary dialogues. A classic example can be found in the journal of the French novelist George Sand: she maintained a regular conversation between her feminine self and an imaginary man, Dr. Piffoel, who represented what she regarded as the male side of her personality.

This process of personification was picked up by F. S. Perls and his fellow Gestalt therapists, who make extensive use of dialogue as a way of reintegrating separated parts of the personality. But, as you will have gathered from the above, this is only one of the possible uses of dialogue. You can use it to talk to parts of your body, your inadequacies, or your unconscious (via 'voices' detected in your journal). You can personify your pets, your belongings, your work. Going beyond yourself, you can use dialogue as a means of exploring your relationship with members of your family, with friends, colleagues, and enemies. Anyone whom you regard as an important factor (whether for good or bad) in your life is a candidate for dialogue. Once again, God (whether as Father, Jesus Christ, Holy Spirit, or all three at once) is an obvious candidate for dialogue in a spiritual journal.[1] Your preachers, your pastor, your role models: the list is endless.

Does it seem silly? Or perhaps you are wondering how to overcome your natural inhibitions against talking to yourself (even if only on paper).

Dialogue is really a brief excursion into fantasy. Allow yourself time and silence to identify with each party to the dialogue before he, she or it speaks. Then just let it flow from the pen onto the paper: write the first thing that comes into your head and, once you have started, try to keep writing as fast as you can (the trick is to write too fast to allow yourself to reflect on and edit what you are writing).

You may find that the dialogue turns into a conversation between several voices. If so, just carry on. It is better to let the situation continue than to interrupt the dialogue in order to think about the identities of the extra voices. When the conversation winds itself up naturally (or it is interrupted by pressure of time) you will be able to reflect on what has happened at leisure. It may be that several of the voices actually belong to the same character. Or, it may be that the issues you have been dealing with cannot be treated satisfactorily without taking others into consideration.

On occasion you may not be sure of the identity of the character with whom you are dialoguing. It may be a stranger in a vivid dream. If this is the case, try concentrating instead on the issue or emotion which has given rise to the urge to dialogue and listen for whatever voices seem to arise.

The Journal as Time Machine
I have already commented that journal entries need not be limited to the present. The recording of significant memories is only the beginning of what can be done in the way of reflecting on your past and future with the aid of your journal.

The journal may be used as a vehicle for exploring your autobiography or personal myth (i.e., the significant past rather than the chronological past). Once again there are no rules. You may choose to write an extensive autobiography or meditation on your journey through life to the present. Or you may prefer to do it in headline form (Ira Progoff's Steppingstones): an eight- or ten-item list of the most important events (internal or external) in your life. If you like, these could be the chapter headings for the book of your life. As usual the most important piece of advice is to do it rapidly (speed inhibits conscious editing, enabling the selection to be a genuine reflection of those events which are currently of

[1] A good example of a dialogue with God is Audrey Dunn's 'Talking with God in the Green Fertile Valley' in *Walking on the Water: Women talk about Spirituality* edited by Jo Garcia and Sara Maitland (Virago), pp 127-31.

most importance to you). Then or at a later date you may pick out items from this list for further examination (perhaps by means of the dialogue technique).

Another possibility is to focus on specific aspects of your life. You may want to record the history of a relationship that was important to you. Or it may be the history of a job, or the history of your relationship with God (in theological jargon: your personal salvation history).

An aspect of reflection on your past which overlaps with the portrait and dialogue sections is imaginary-ancestor-hunting. Most of us at one time or another have taken some sort of interest in our ancestry. In your journal you are free to daydream about those people you would like to have had as ancestors. Who are your spiritual ancestors? Your intellectual ancestors? Who has inspired you? Who has influenced you? An imaginary genealogy could be the starting point for a series of dialogues exploring the ways in which a variety of people have left their mark on your personality.

You may also use the journal to explore your future. This can take the form of a specific examination of the various possibilities offered by an important life choice you have to make. Take a career decision for example. Imagine yourself in each of the possible situations in turn. Build up a mental picture of what it would be like. Then write a diary entry for a date several years hence, reflecting on what you are now doing, how it has affected you and those around you. You may then went to explore this further by dialoguing with each of your future selves.

Alternatively it can be less specific. You might like to imagine what would happen if you were to win a fortune, or lose your job, or be told that you have terminal cancer. What would your response be? Reflecting on such matters may reveal to you action that you may want to take now (like writing a will). Or, it may throw up aspects of your personality that you need to come to terms with.

Similar in vein to the last paragraph would be reflection on your death. You might consider writing an imaginary obituary. Or you would prepare a fantasy will (a journal is also a useful place for working on the practical details of a real will). Or you might like to write your funeral and think about why you have chosen the items in it.

Some Graphic Exercises
It is not always possible to express yourself in words. In fact, it is usually impossible to say exactly what you want to say. For this reason, many people find themselves resorting to doodles, diagrams and drawings in their journals. Here are a few suggestions for drawings you might like to try out as the basis for self-examination.

(a) A MAP OF SOUL COUNTRY: Take a page in your journal and draw on it a map representing your inner life. Once you have drawn in the outline you can fill it in with as few or as many topographical details as you like, e.g., the forest of confusion about what I believe, or the cliffs of withdrawal. Try to be as specific as possible about the names of these features. The result may be very different from the image you try to project of yourself. As you can imagine, such a map, because it expresses so much in such a condensed form, can become the basis for a considerable amount of journalling. Try describing each of the features in greater detail. Prepare a tour guide for your soul.

(b) BODY MAPPING: Draw an outline picture of yourself without your clothes. How do you feel about it? Embarrassed? Write about your reactions. Mark on the map the places about which you feel embarrassed; the parts at which you usually experience pain, energy, excitement, expectation, tiredness. Write about each of these in turn.

(c) WHAT TIME IS IT?: Draw a clockface and after reflecting on it, draw in the hands of the clock to show what time it is in your life. You might like to put events and goals around the circumstance. From this you can go on to prepare lists completing the following sentences: It is too late for. . . It is too early for . . . It is time for . . .

(d) THE WHEEL OF LIFE: Draw a wheel to represent all the concerns, interests, and commitments in your life. Place those that occur to you at what seem to be the appropriate distance from the centre. As you do this exercise, you may find that the priorities in your life become clearer.

(e) ROAD MAP: If life is a journey, then it can be represented diagrammatically by a road map. Try drawing a map showing where you have come from (literally or figuratively) and where you are going. Mark in the points you have visited or will visit en route. As always, start by reflecting on the exercise, then carry it out quickly, marking in whatever comes to mind. You may surprise yourself.

Specialist Lists
A number of lists have already been mentioned in the preceding sections. I will mention just one more, which I have found to be particularly useful in uncovering, and making me face up to, my prejudices. This list is headed Them and Us. In one column you list all those who you are comfortable with. In the other column you list those who make you uncomfortable. When the list is complete you can then begin to examine why you have placed particular individuals or groups of people in one column rather than another. What do you like about those in the 'Us' column? What do you dislike about those in the 'Them' column? Which of these features might an observer be able to detect in your own personality? What good features can you think of for each of the entries in the 'Them' column?

Journalling as a Community Experience
While on the subject of further journalling exercises and experiments it is worth bearing in mind the potential for a community journal or a family journal. Many of us keep family or parish photograph albums and scrapbooks. It is but a small step from that to a family, church or community journal. George Simons mentions one particularly interesting example called the Hub-bub which circulates around various members of a large and scattered family in the U.S.A. It is a way of maintaining the identity of the family.

You may like to begin by either keeping a family journal for the next summer holiday, or as a family, creating a short tribute scrapbook of a relative who has recently died. It can be a way of sharing the process of grieving with thanksgiving, mutual support and hope.

5. FURTHER RESOURCES

(a) Books about Journalling

Christina Baldwin, *One To One: Self-Understanding Through Journal Writing* (M. Evans, New York).

Milt Hughes, *Spiritual Journey Notebook* (National Student Ministries, Nashville).
An explicitly evangelical contribution to the art of journalling. It is too directive for my taste: a sort of Christian Fil-o-fax.

Morton Kelsey, *Adventure Inwards: Christian Growth Through Personal Journal Writing* (Augsburg Publishing House, Minneapolis).

Marion Milner, *An Experiment In Leisure* (Virago Press).
A Life Of One's Own (Virago Press).
Eternity's Sunrise: A Way Of Keeping A Diary (Virago Press).

Ira Progoff, *At A Journal Workshop* (Dialogue House, New York).
The Practice Of Process Meditation (Dialogue House, New York)

Tristine Rainer, *The New Diary* (Angus & Robertson).
She offers a simpler and more flexible approach to journalling than Progoff. It is unashamedly secular but many of the exercises can be adapted for use as spiritual exercises.

George F. Simons, *Keeping Your Personal Journal* (Paulist Press).
An excellent Roman Catholic introduction to journalling as a spiritual exercise.

(b) Examples of Spiritual Journals

George Bernanos, *Diary of a Country Priest* (Fount).

E. M. Blaiklock, *Kathleen* (Hodder and Stoughton).

Alexander Elchaninov, *Diary of a Russian Priest* (SVS Press).

Elisabeth Elliott (ed.), *The Journals of Jim Elliott* (Pickering & Inglis).

George Fox, *Journal* (Cambridge University Press).

Dag Hammarskjold, *Markings* (Faber).

Soren Kierkegaard, *The Journals 1834-1854* (Fontana).
The Last Years: Journals 1853-55 (Fontana).

C. S. Lewis, *A Grief Observed* (Faber).

Thomas Merton, *The Asian Journal* (Sheldon Press).

Henri Nouwen, *The Genesee Diary* (Doubleday).
Gracias: A Latin American Journal (Harper & Row).

Pope John XXIII, *Journal of a Soul* (Chapman).

Roger Schutz, Prior of Taize: six volumes of his personal journal have been published under various titles by Mowbrays.

John Michael Talbot, *Changes* (Crossroad Publishing, Co.).

George Whitefield, *Journals* (Banner of Truth).

John Woolman, *The Journal and Major Essays* (Oxford University Press).

(c) Other Journals (Fact and Fiction) which may be of interest

Charles Darwin, *The Voyage of the 'Beagle'* (Dent).

Lawrence Durrell, *The Black Book* (E. P. Dutton).

Anne Frank, *The Diary* (Pan Books).

Andre Gide, *Journals* (Penguin).

Etty Hillesum, *Etty: A Diary 1941-43* (Granada).

Doris Lessing, *The Golden Notebook* (Michael Joseph).
Katherine Mansfield, *The Journal* (Constable).
Anais Nin, *The Diary*, 6 volumes (Harcourt, Brace & World).
Adrian Plass, *The Sacred Diary of Adrian Plass (aged 37¼)* (Marshall-Pickering).
Beatrix Potter, *Journal, 1881-1897* (abridged) (Warne).
Henri Thoreau, *The Journal* (University of Chicago Press).
Sue Townsend, *The Secret Diary of Adrian Mole, Aged 13¾.*

(d) Other Books which may be worth consulting
Gerard W. Hughes, *God of Surprises* (Darton, Longman & Todd).
Morton Kelsey, *The Other Side of Silence* (Paulist Press).
Una Kroll, *The Spiritual Exercise Book* (Firethorn Press).
Mark Link, *You: Prayer For Beginners and Those Who Have Forgotten How* (Argus).
Anthony de Mello, *Sadhana: A Way to God* (Doubleday).
Russ Parker, *Dreams and Spirituality* (Grove Spirituality Series No. 15).
Roger Pooley, *Spiritual Autobiography: A DIY Guide* (Grove Spirituality Series No. 4).
Louis J. Puhl (translator), *The Spiritual Exercises of St. Ignatius* (Loyola University Press).

(e) Workshops
Information about journalling workshops is obtainable from:
Emmaus House, Clifton Hill, Clifton, Bristol BS8 4PD.
Inigo Centre, Southwell House, 39 Fitzjohns Avenue, London, NW3 5JT.
National Retreat Centre, Liddon House, 24 South Audley Street, London, W1Y 5DL.
Post Green Community, 56 Dorchester Road, Lytchett Minster, Poole, Dorset BH16 6JE.

POSTSCRIPT

Some people dismiss journalling as pathologically introspective. Because the journal is concened primaily with oneself they think it panders to human self-centredness. While I cannot deny that some journal keepers tend to be unhealthily absorbed in themselves, I do not believe that this is a serious danger for anyone who is honestly trying to keep a spiritual journal. If you make a habit of examining yourself in God's presence, you will find that he keeps drawing you away from self-absorption towards a greater concern for your neighbours and a greater awareness of his glory.

I have found journalling to be a very valuable spiritual exercise. My hope is that this booklet will have encouraged you to experiment with the techniques for yourself.